Clare Beaton's

MAKE AND COLOUR

PAPER DINOSAURS

b small publishing

How to use this book

• First remove the centre black and white pages of the book. These are dinosaurs and vegetation ready for you to colour.

• Place the book on a flat surface and ask an adult to help you open the staples. Pull out the pages carefully, then close the staples again.

• Colour the outlined shapes on both sides. Use coloured pencils, crayons, felt-tip pens or paints.

• Cut out the shapes once they are coloured, and slot the legs and bodies together.

• Keep the rest of the book. It has lots of ideas on how to make other things. There are also templates and stencils to help you.

Some things you will need:

- black and white paper or thin card
- cardboard boxes and tubes
- newspaper
- scissors, craft knife
- tracing paper
- pencil, ruler
- masking tape, sticky tape, glue
- crayons, paints and felt-tip pens
- darning needle and thread

This symbol is to remind you to ask an adult to help when you use a craft knife.

Paint effects

Dinosaurs most likely had scaly skin like reptiles. Some were armour-plated. No one really knows what colour they were, but many were probably camouflaged in colour and pattern to help them hide from their predators. See below for some ideas on how to paint your dinosaurs.

Sponging

Paint one fairly thick coat and, while it is still wet, dab it with scrunched-up kitchen towel to create a dappled effect. Or, paint one coat and let it dry. Then dip kitchen towel into a saucer of a contrasting or darker paint. Dab on to the first coat.

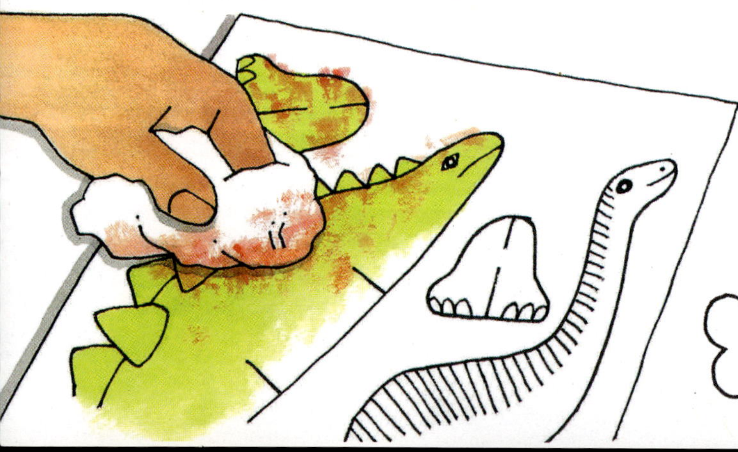

Scaly patterns

Colour the dinosaur in one colour. If you use paint, leave it to dry. Add a pattern in a contrasting colour. Cut a zigzag, wavy or scalloped edge along a piece of stiff paper. Place it on the dinosaur and colour up to the edge. Move the card along and repeat to create a stripy, scaly effect.

Templates

Here is a way to trace from the templates on the inside of the front and back covers very simply and successfully.

What you will need:

- tracing paper
- sticky tape
- soft pencil
- paper or card

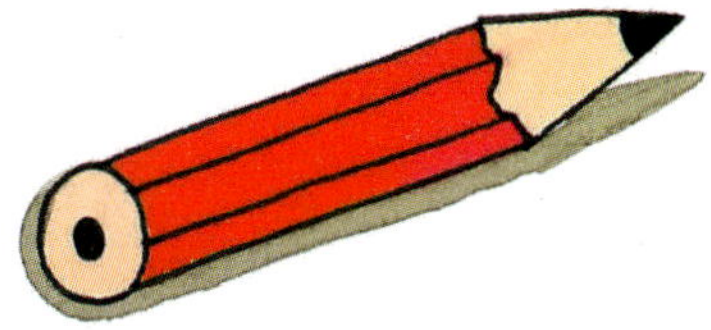

Tape a piece of tracing paper over the template. Trace the shape with the pencil.

Turn over the tracing paper and scribble over the lines with the pencil.

Turn over again and tape on to some card or paper. Retrace firmly over the lines. Remove the tracing paper.

Stencils

Cut or tear off the sheet of stencils from the back cover. Follow the instructions below on how to use them.

What you will need:

- paper or card (coloured if you want)
- pencil
- scissors

Place the stencil shape on some card or paper. Draw inside the shape with a pencil.

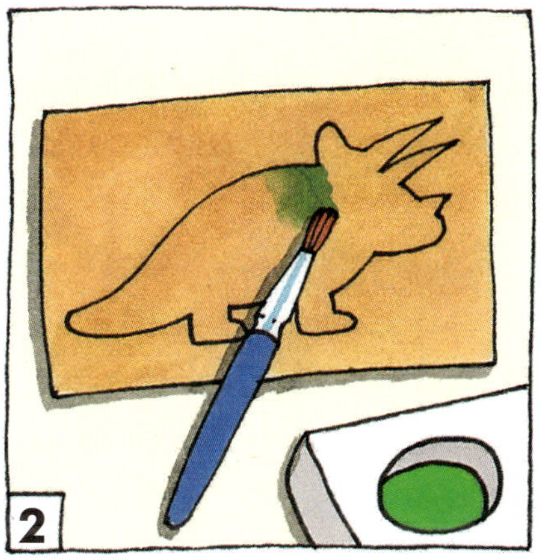

Colour in the outline shape or cut it out with scissors.

Palaeolithic panoramas

Make some background scenery for your animals out of a cardboard box.

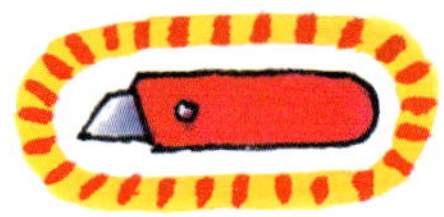

First, cut off one side of the box.

Then cut off the flaps at the top and bottom.

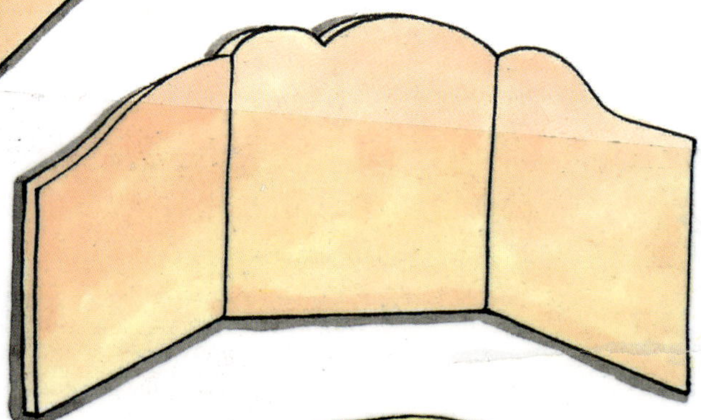

Draw a curvy line along the top of the card. Cut the top off along the line.

Draw your own prehistoric landscape in pencil. Then colour or paint it in lush bright greens. You could paint an erupting volcano in fiery red colours.

Use the fern templates inside the front cover. See how to trace them on page 3.

Ferns

Trace ferns from the inside front cover on to stiff paper and cut them out. Paint or colour them on both sides. Stick them into a lump of modelling clay to stand them up.

If you don't want to cut out the space between the leaves, paint it dark green and cut around the whole leaf.

Tree ferns

Paint a small card tube brown to make a tree trunk. Stick ferns inside the top with sticky tape or glue.

Boulders

Scrunch up a sheet of newspaper and tape it together with masking tape. Paint it in grey or brown. You could make lots of them in different sizes.

Desert

Spread glue on to paper or card. Sprinkle it with dry sand. Shake off the excess. Or use sandpaper!

Scary silhouettes

Paint some paper in bright stripes of yellow, red, pink and orange for a hot volcanic background. Leave to dry.

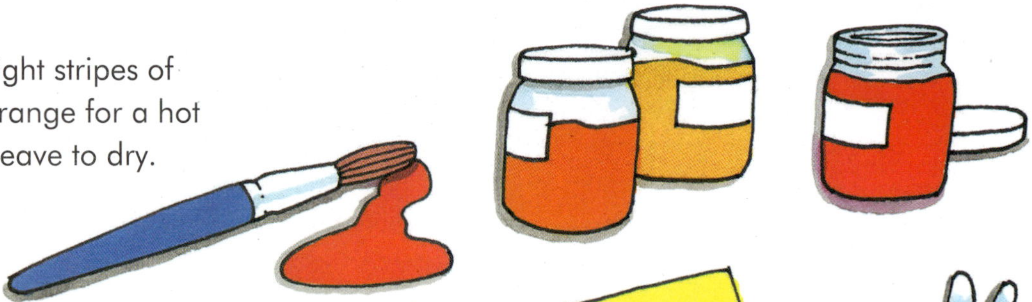

Cut land shapes out of black paper and glue them in place.

Use the stencils to draw some dinosaurs and vegetation on to black paper.

Cut them out and glue them on top of the land shapes, to your own design.

Glue the pterodactylus in the sky and the elasmosaurus in the water.

See page 3 for how to use the stencils on the back cover flap.

Frieze

Make a frieze to decorate your bedroom. Cut a strip of paper 12 cm wide and as long as you like. Paint it in bright, hot colours. When dry, glue a 2-cm strip of black paper along the bottom.

Draw some stencil shapes on to black paper. Cut them out and glue them along the black strip.

Dinosaur cards

Fold some pieces of thin white card in two, to make cards.

Paint the front colourfully, as before. When dry, glue a dinosaur silhouette on it.

Alternatively, paint some white paper in bright hot colours, then use the stencils to cut shapes out of it. Glue them on to black paper cards.

Cut out a circle for a sun.

Prehistoric puppets

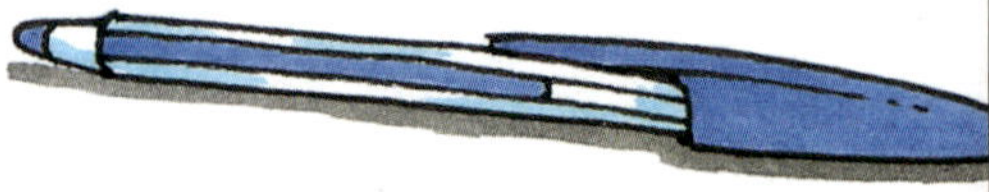

Place the stencil on to a double thickness of green felt (pin together). Draw a shape carefully in biro. Cut along the biro line, through both thicknesses.

Spread glue on to one side of one of the pieces, as shown by the darker green area on the drawing to the right. Leave a shape for your finger and do not glue the legs.

Place the second dinosaur shape on top of the first and press them together. Decorate your puppet with sequins or felt shapes.

Puppet stand

Cut a length of stiff paper with three (or more) finger shapes on top, to stand your puppets on. Use the template below to help. See page 3 for how to trace the template.

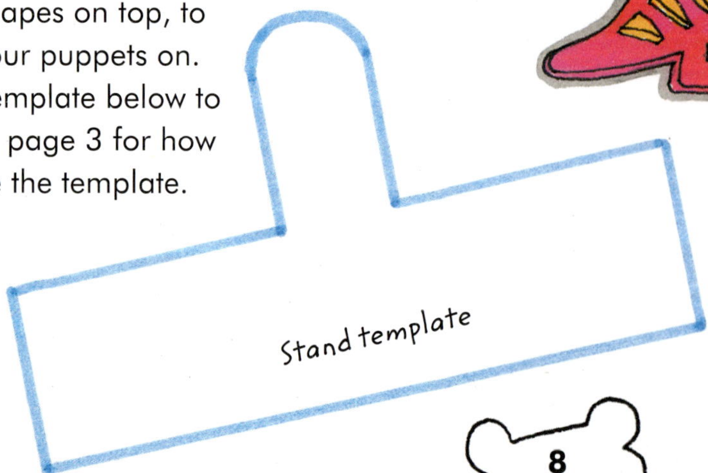

Fold the stand into a zigzag and use it to hold your finger puppets.